Learning the Bass
Book One

For Individual Study, Single-String Classes, or Mixed-String Classes

Expanded Edition

by Cassia Harvey

CHP283

C. Harvey Publications

©2015 by C. Harvey Publications   All Rights Reserved.

www.charveypublications.com

Warmup Exercise for the Beginning of Class

0 1 4 1 4 1 4 1

0 1 4 1 4 1 4 1

0 1 4 1 4 1 4 1

0 1 4 1 4 1 4 1

0

Play this exercise on all four strings.
Use it as a warmup every time you play.

1. Parts of the Bass and Bow

Bass

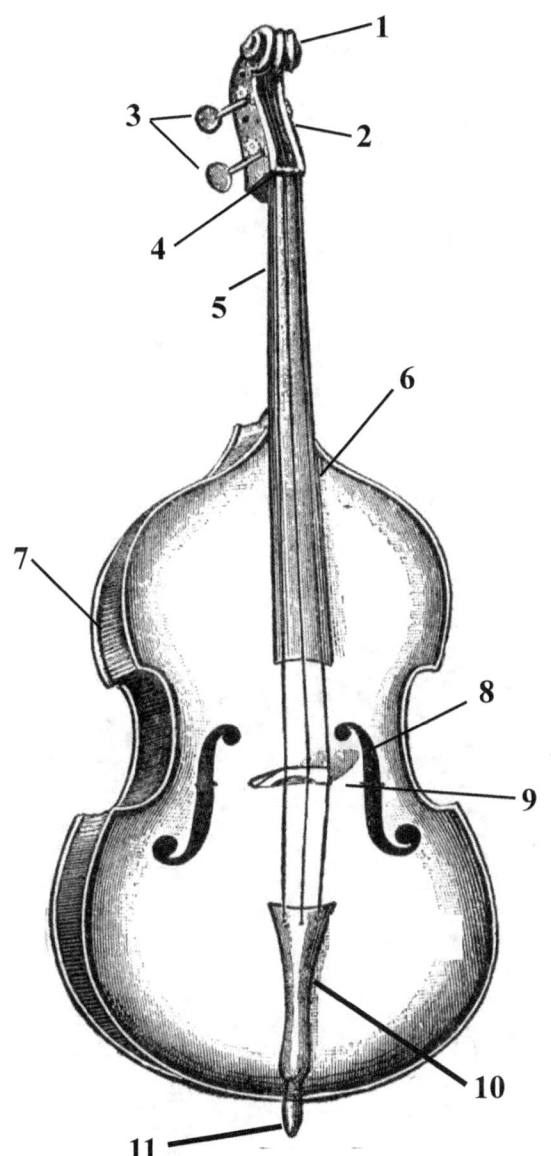

1. scroll
2. peg box
3. pegs
4. nut
5. neck
6. fingerboard
7. sides
8. f holes
9. bridge
10. tailpiece
11. endpin

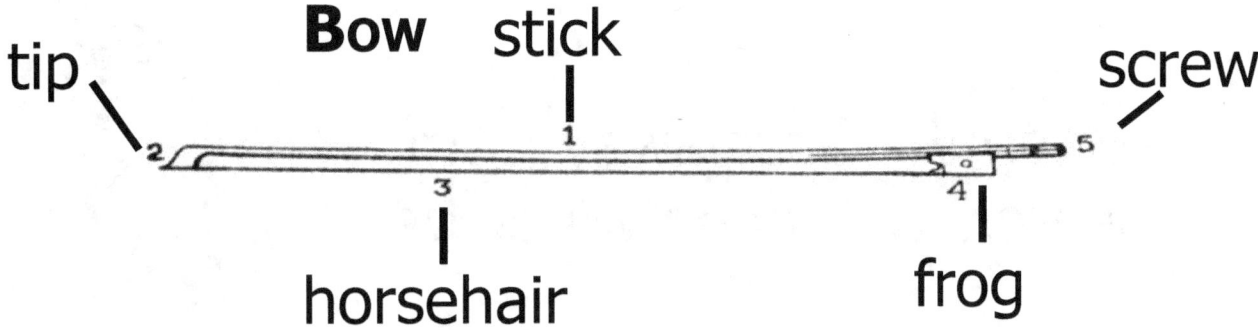

©2015 C. Harvey Publications All Rights Reserved.

2. Taking care of the Bass

Keep your bass away from pets.

Don't let the bass drop
(or the bow).

The wood is very fragile.

No water on the bass or bow.

Keep the bass away from heaters and open windows.

3. Taking care of the Bow

Don't touch the bow hair!

Righty-tighty: To tighten the bow, turn the screw to the right.

Lefty-loosey: To loosen the bow, turn the screw to the left.

Always loosen the bow when you are finished playing.

Keep the bass and bow up off the floor.

4. The Open Strings

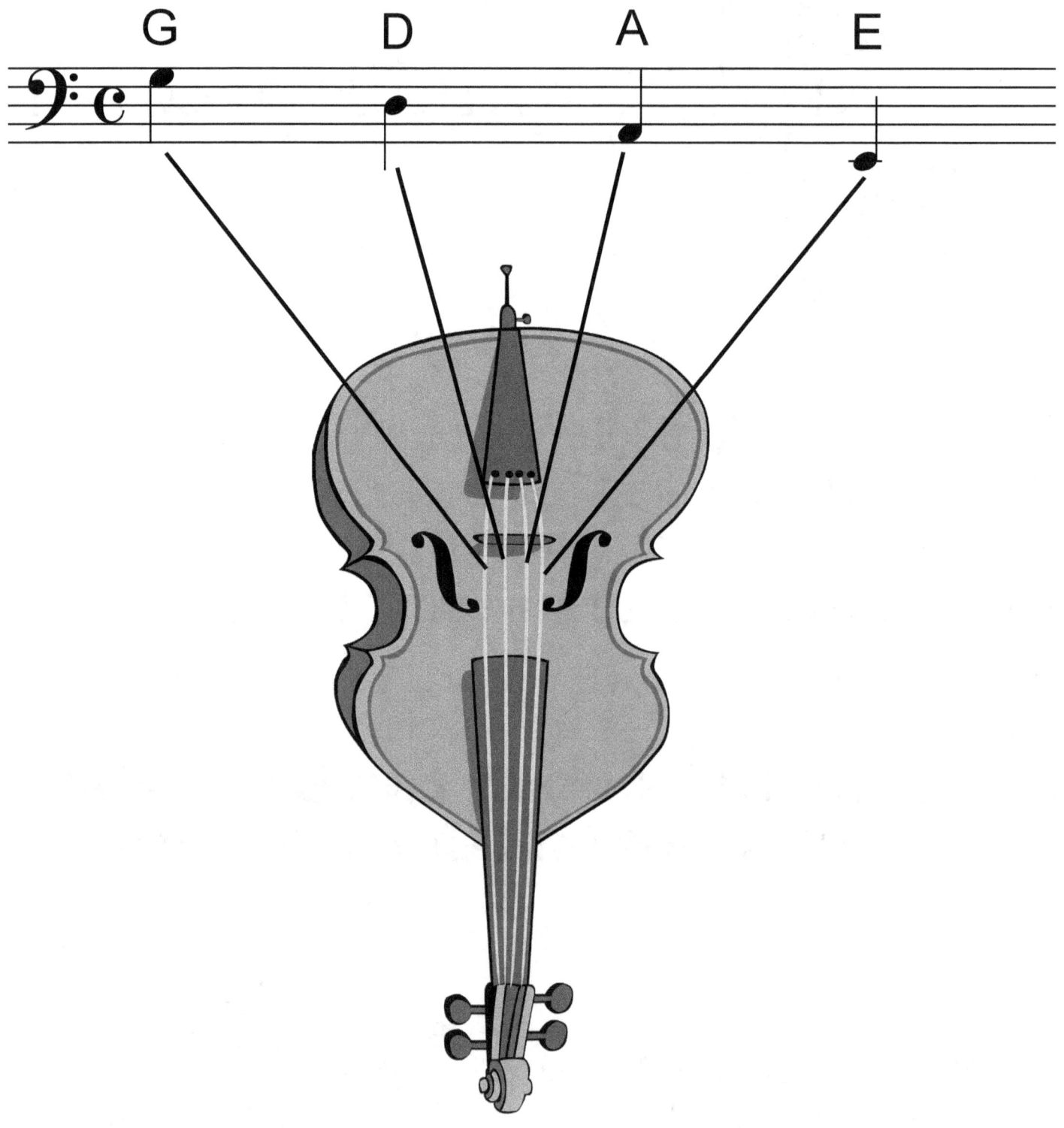

5. Pluck the Open Strings

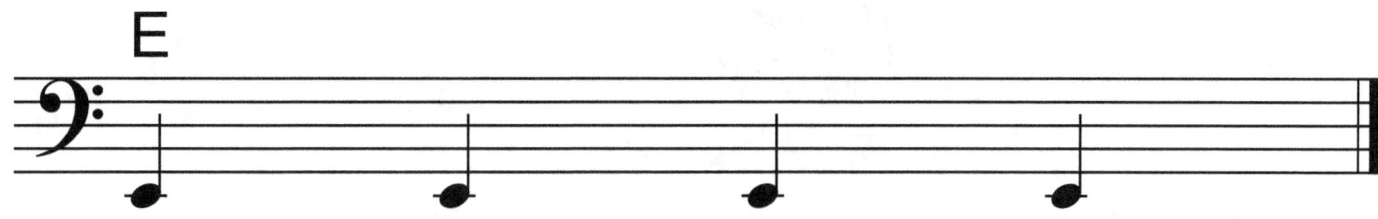

6. Open String Song

play with long bows, from the frog to the tip

GGGG   DDDD   AAAA   EEEE

EEEE   AAAA   DDDD   GGGG

GG DD AA EE   EE AA DD GG

GDGD   DADA   AEAE   EADG

7. Mississippi Hot Dog

4 short bows and 2 long bows

Play the rhythm "Mississippi Hot Dog" on each note:

G G D D   A A E E

G D A E   E A D G

G D   D A   A E   E A

8. Blueberry Song:
Long-Short-Short

G - GG   G - GG

D - DD   D - DD

A - AA   A - AA

E - EE   E - EE

A - AA   A - AA

D - DD   D - DD

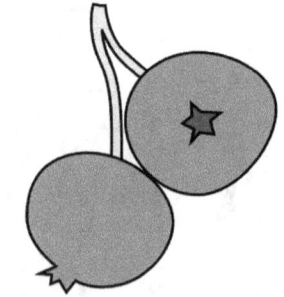

9. Speedy Open Strings

AAAA   EEEE

AAAA   DDDD

GGGG   DDDD

AAEE   AAEE

AADD   AADD

GGDD   GGDD

10. The Finger Numbers

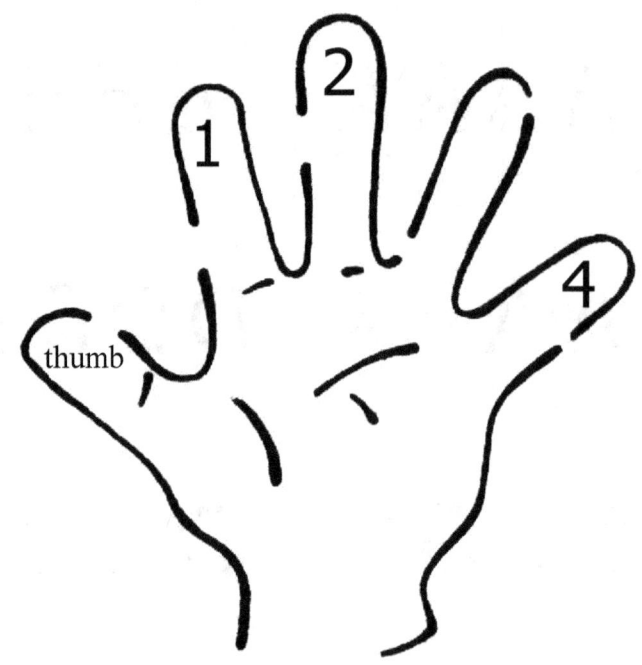

Using the Fingers

0 is for open string
1 is for first finger
2 is for second finger
4 is for fourth finger
The thumb goes under the neck of the bass.

11. First Finger Song

0000   1111   0000   1111

00 11 00 11   1111   0000

String Class: Play on the A string or D string.
Solo: Can be played on all 4 strings.

12. First Finger Challenge

0011   0011   0000   1111

0011   1100   1111   0000

0101   0000   0101   0000

©2015 C. Harvey Publications All Rights Reserved.

13. Fourth Finger Song

0000　　1111　　4444　　1111

0000　　1111　　4444　　1111

00　11　44　11　00　11　44　11　00

String Class: Play on the A string or D string.
Solo: Can be played on all 4 strings.

14. Fourth Finger Challenge!

11 00　11 44　11 44　1111

44 11　4141　4141　0000

15. Hot Cross Buns

410 -   410 -

0000   1111

410 -

String Class: Play on the A string or D string.
Solo: Can be played on all 4 strings.

16. Au clair de la Lune

0001   4 - 1 -   0411   0 ---

0001   4 - 1 -   0411   0 ---

17. Mary Had a Little Lamb

String Class: Play on the A string or D string.
Solo: Can be played on all 4 strings.

4 1 0 1

4 4 4 -

1 1 1 -

4 4 4 -

4 1 0 1

4 4 4 4

1 1 4 1

0 - - -

18. Another Fourth Finger Song

0000　　1111　　4444　　1111

4444　　1111　　4444　　1111

00　11　44　11　44　11　44　11　00

String Class: Play on the A string or D string.
Solo: Can be played on all 4 strings.

19. Another Fourth Finger Challenge!

11 44　11 44　11 44 11 44

44 11　41 41　00 11 41 41

20. Finger Training

D string	G string
0 1 4	0 1 0 1 0

G string	D string
1 0 4	1 0 1 0 1

D string	G string
0 1 4	0 1 0 1 0

G string	D string
1 0 4	1 0 1 0 1

D string

4 1 4 1   4 1 4 1 0

©2015 C. Harvey Publications All Rights Reserved.

Learning the Bass, Book One

21a. Ode to Joy

Beethoven

D string | G string | D string
4 4 | 0 1 1 0 | 4 1

0 0 1 4 4 1 1 -

G string | D string
4 4 | 0 1 1 0 | 4 1

0 0 1 4 1 0 0 -

Can you figure out the rest?

©2015 C. Harvey Publications All Rights Reserved.

21b. Special Challenge: Ode to Joy, Second Part

22. Rests

This sign is called a quarter rest:

When you see a rest like this, stop playing and count to 1 before playing again.

String Class: Play on the A string or the D string.
Solo: Can be played on all 4 strings.

23. Au clair de la Lune

0 0 0 1 4 𝄽 1 𝄽

0 4 1 1 0 𝄽 𝄽 𝄽

Repeat

Breaking the notes up

Now we break the notes up with a line: |

24. Purcell's Rigaudon

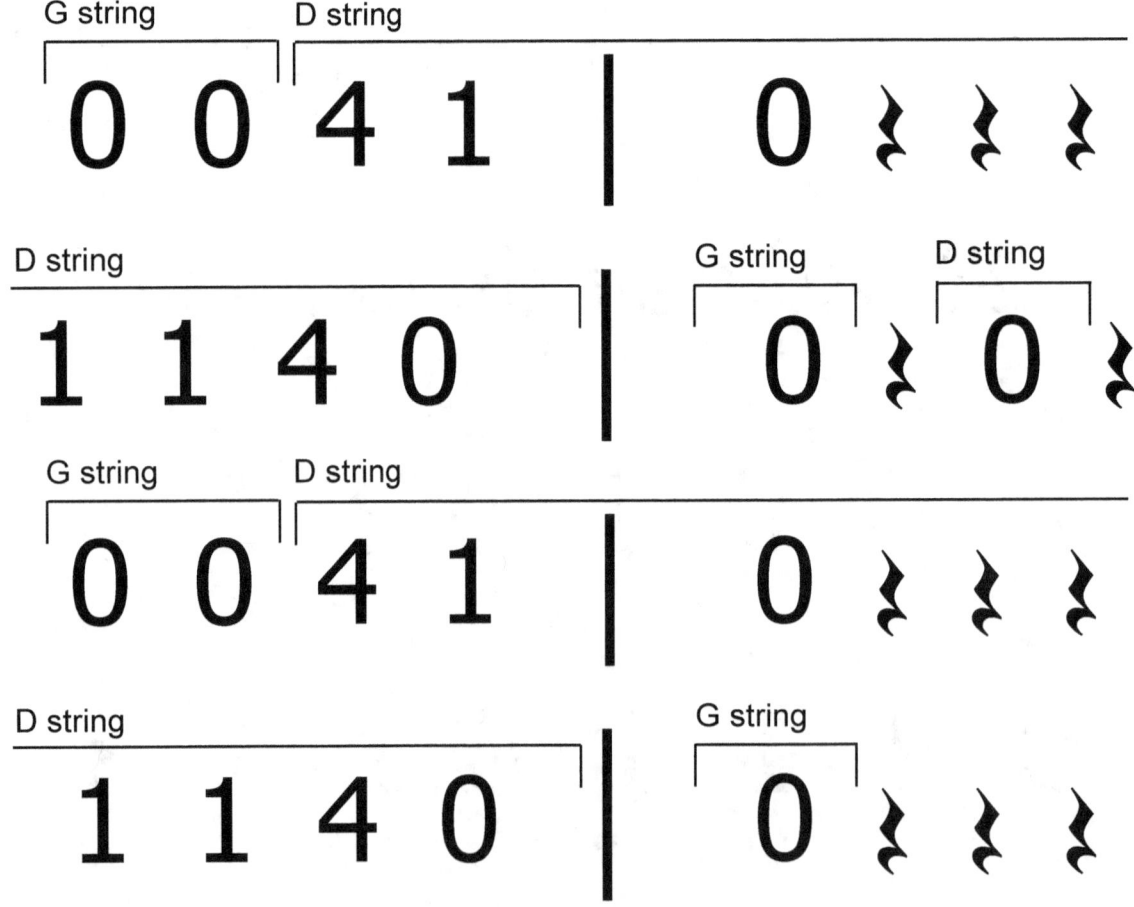

25. A Regal March
(Start on the D String. "G" means open G.)

| 0014 | GG44 | 0014 | 1100 |

| 0014 | GG44 | 0014 | 1100 |

26. Three-Leaf Clover

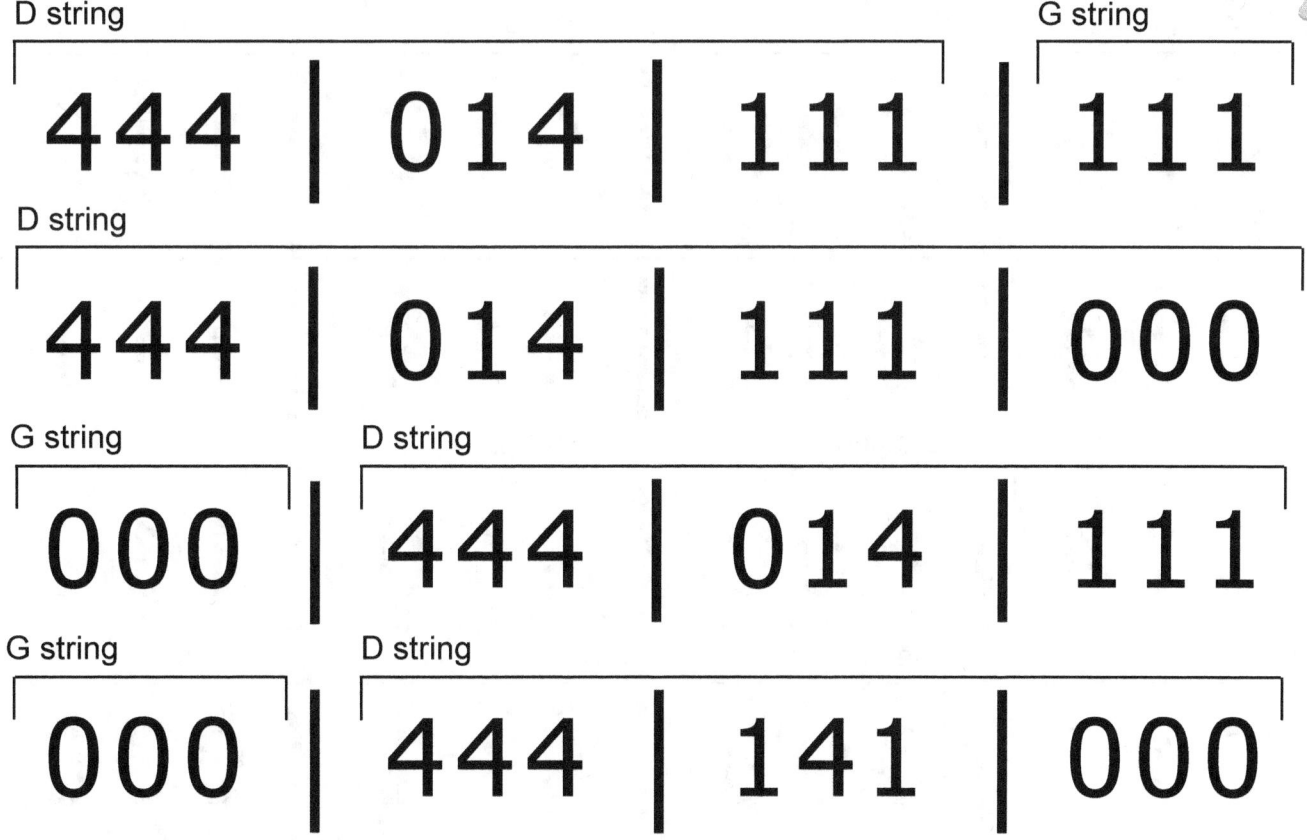

D string ————————————————— G string
| 444 | 014 | 111 | 111 |

D string ————————————————————
| 444 | 014 | 111 | 000 |

G string   D string ————————————
| 000 | 444 | 014 | 111 |

G string   D string ————————————
| 000 | 444 | 141 | 000 |

27. Falling Down!

D string	G string	D string	
4 4 1 0	0 0 4 1	4 0 1 4	1 𝄽 1 𝄽

D string	G string	D string	
4 4 1 0	0 0 4 1	4 0 1 4	1 𝄽 1 𝄽

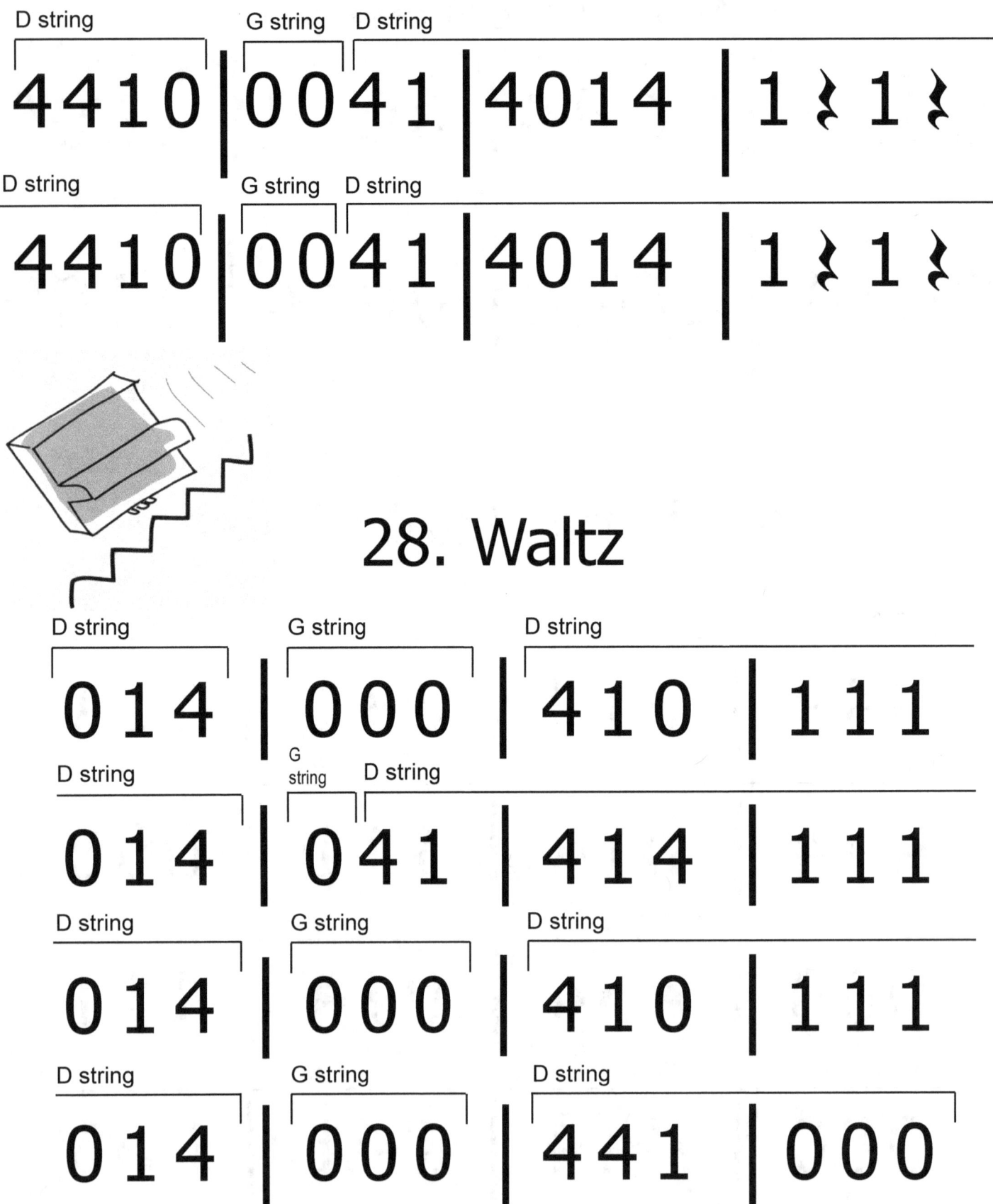

28. Waltz

D string	G string	D string	
0 1 4	0 0 0	4 1 0	1 1 1

D string	G string	D string	
0 1 4	0 4 1	4 1 4	1 1 1

D string	G string	D string	
0 1 4	0 0 0	4 1 0	1 1 1

D string	G string	D string	
0 1 4	0 0 0	4 4 1	0 0 0

29. Reaching Saturn

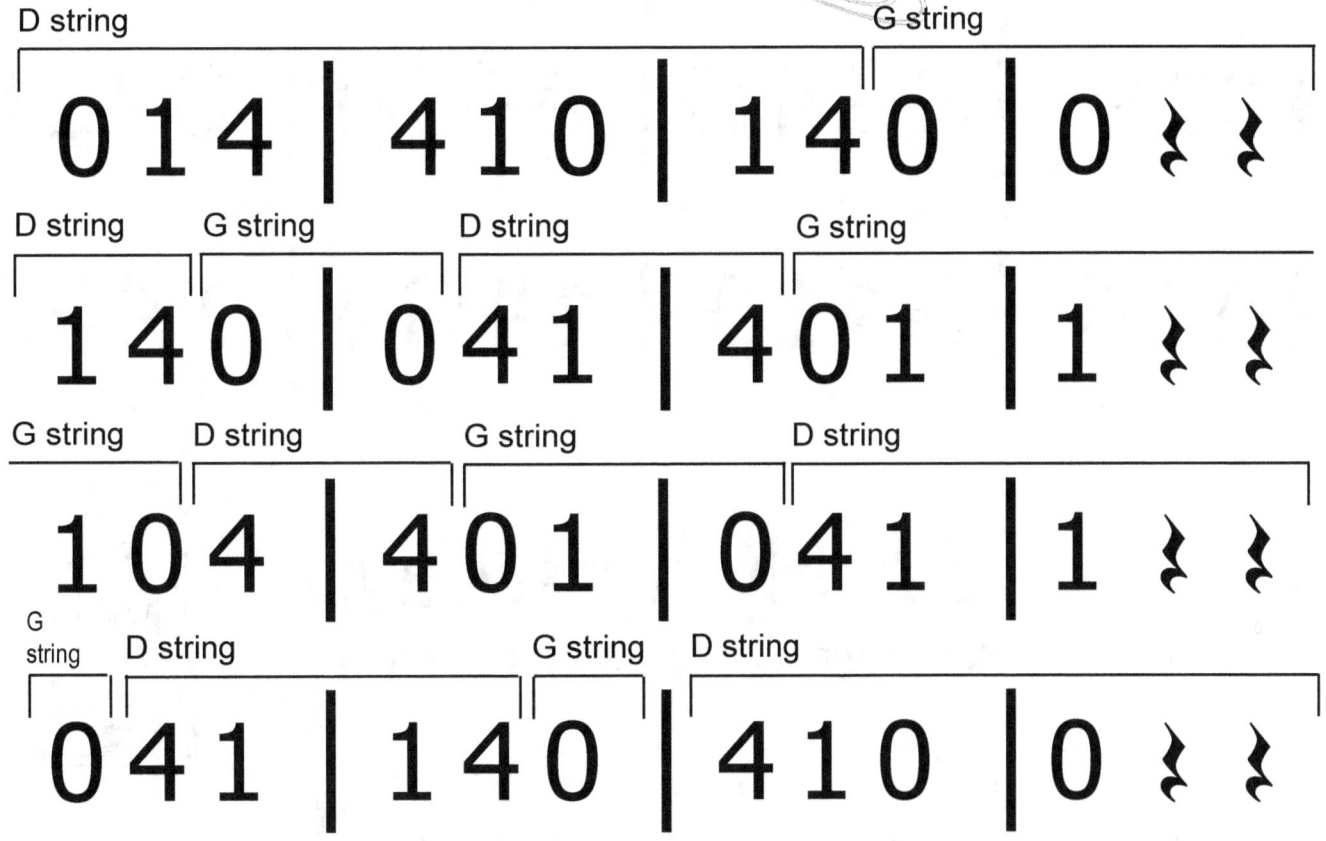

30. Back to Earth
(Start on the D string. "G" means open G.)

0410 | 1111 | 1G41 | 4444

4014 | GGGG | 4G14 | 0000

31. Neptune

(Start on the D string. "G" means open G.)

| 4414 | GG4G | 4414 | 041𝄾 |

| 4414 | G410 | 44G4 | 140𝄾 |

32. Flying Away

(Start on the D string. "G" means open G.)

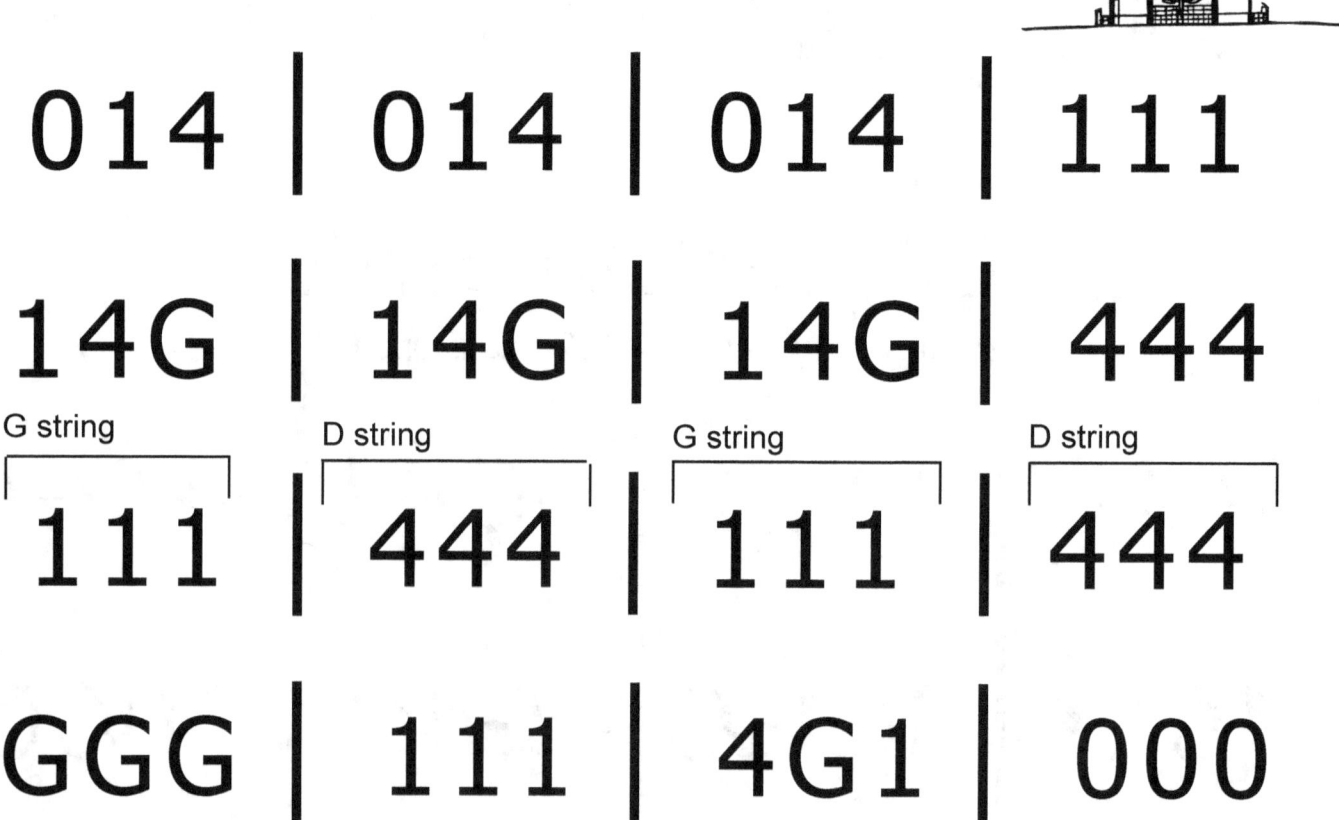

| 014 | 014 | 014 | 111 |

| 14G | 14G | 14G | 444 |

| G string | D string | G string | D string |
| 111 | 444 | 111 | 444 |

| GGG | 111 | 4G1 | 000 |

Learning the Bass, Book One

33. Reading Music

This is a bass clef sign. The bass plays notes in bass clef.

This is a staff. It has 5 lines and 4 spaces. The notes go on the lines and in the spaces.

The music notes are placed on the lines and in the spaces to mean certain sounds.

Line Notes
Good
Boys
Deserve
Fudge
Always

Space Notes
F
A
C
E
Guard

The notes go in order of the alphabet, from A to G, and then start back at A again.

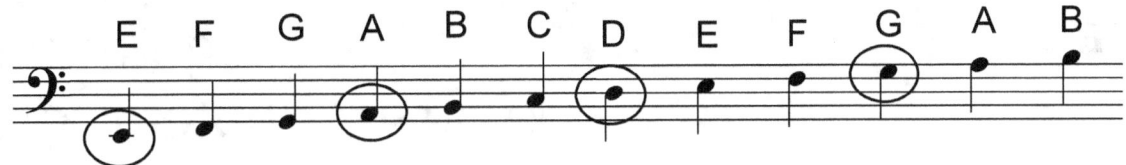

©2015 C. Harvey Publications All Rights Reserved.

34. Counting

♩ This is a quarter note.
Hold it for 1 count.

𝅗𝅥 This is a half note.
Hold it for 2 counts.

𝅝 This is a whole note.
Hold it for 4 counts.

♪ This is an eighth note.
Hold it for 1/2 a count.

Two eighth notes together equal one quarter note (1 count.)

35. A and B on the A String

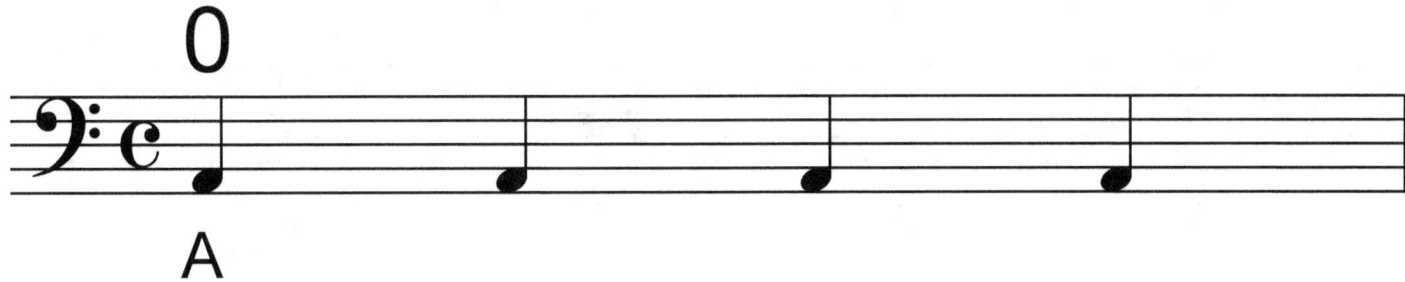
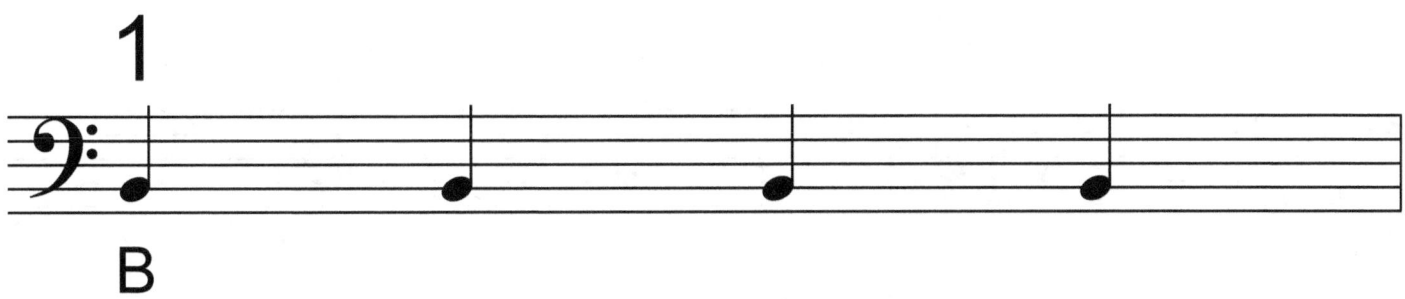
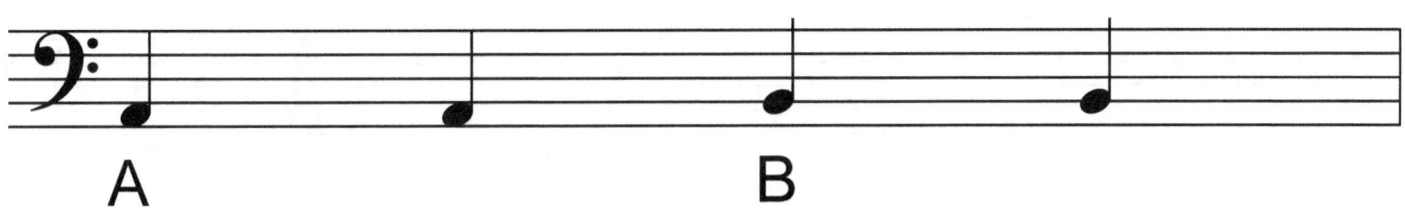
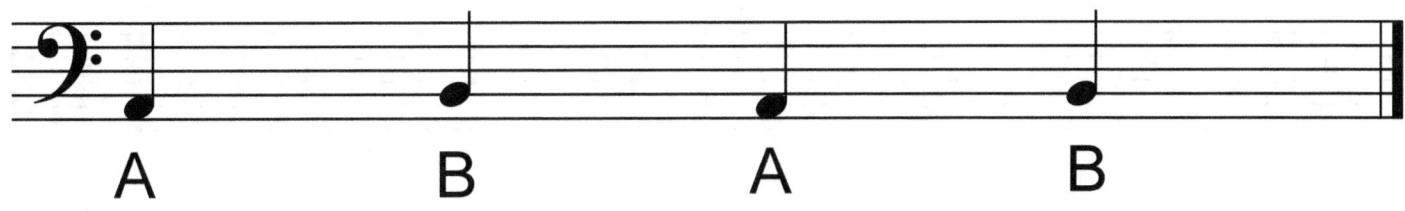

36. A, B, and C♯ on the A String

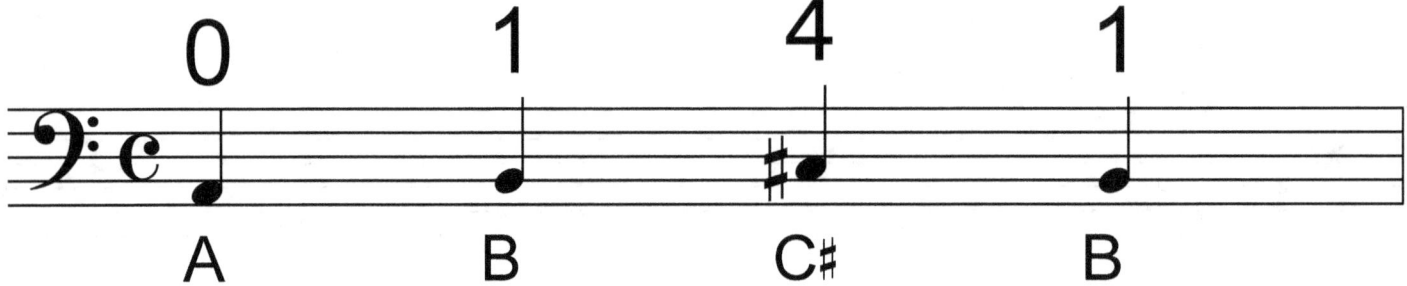

37. The notes A, B, C♯, and D

38. Boil Them Cabbage Down

39. Long-Short-Short Cabbage

40. ♩ Half Notes get 2 Counts

41. Mississippi Hot Dogs with Cabbage

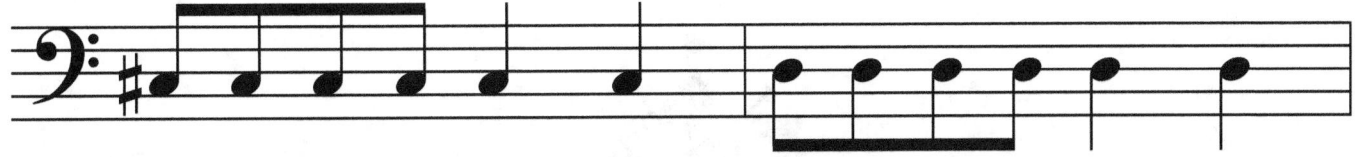

42. Miss Mary Mack

43. D and E on the D String

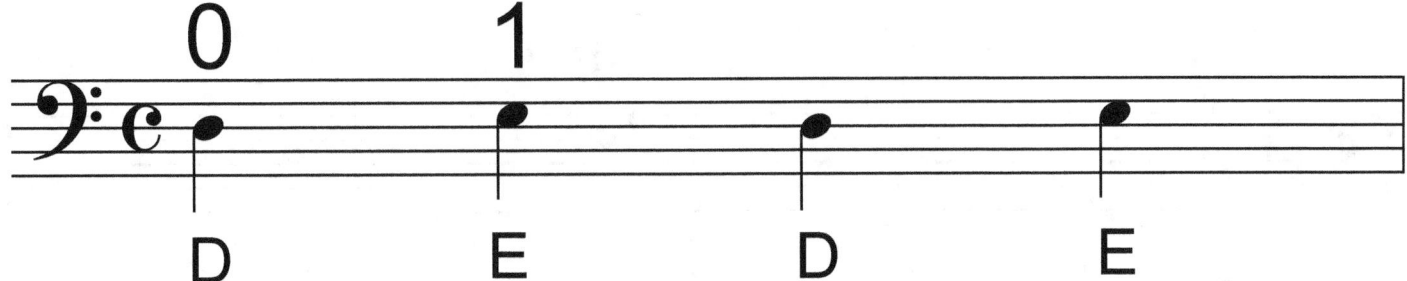

44. D, E, and F♯ on the D String

45. D, E, F#, and G on the D String

46. Pickle Juice, Pickle Juice

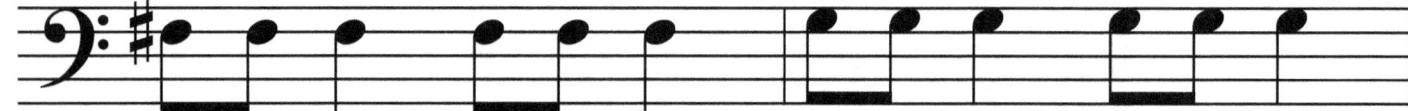

47. Pickle Juice Stomp

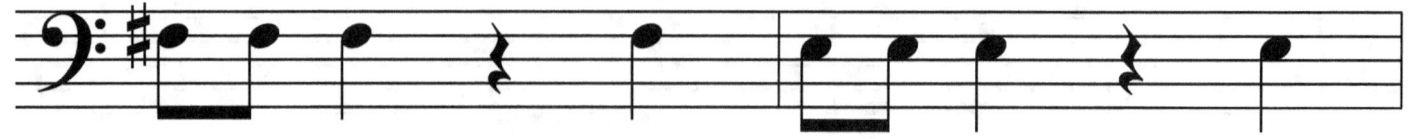

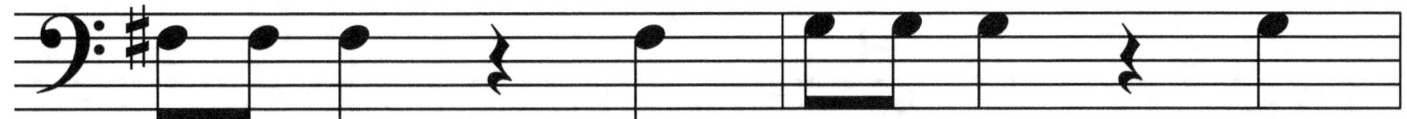

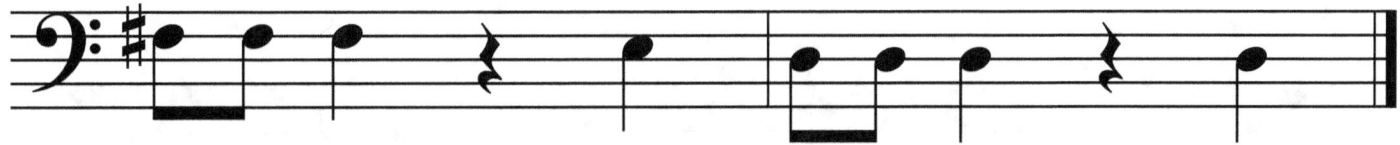

48. Peanut Butter Pie Pickle Juice

49. The Rattle Sna-wa-wake

50. The D string and the G string

51. Playing on D and G

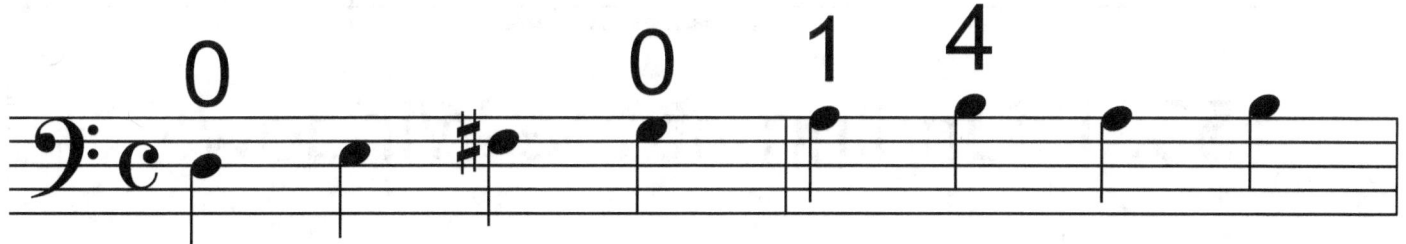

54. Tapping at the Window!

Basses Learn to Shift to 3rd Position

55. The D Major Scale

56. Super Challenge!

57. Twinkle, Twinkle, Little Star

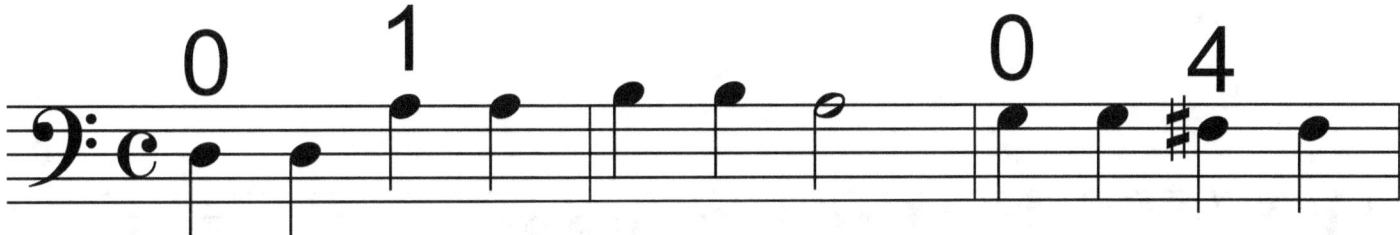

58. Twinkle, Twinkle (Mississippi Hot Dog)

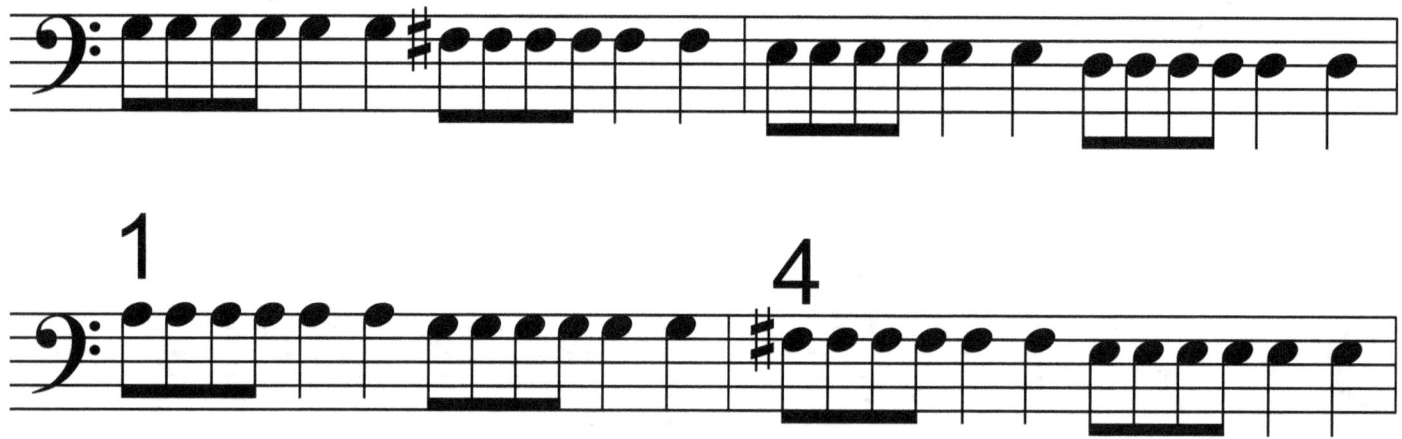

59. Ode to Joy

Beethoven

Basses Learn to Shift to 3rd Position on D

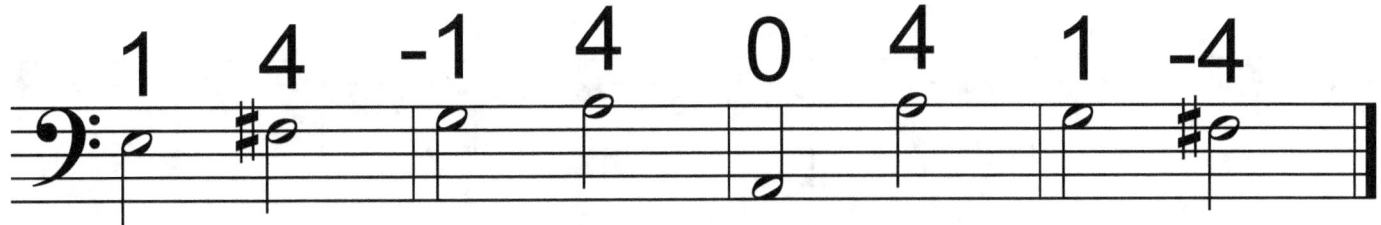

60. Fulton Had a Steamboat

61. Pickle Juice Steamboat

62. Blueberry Steamboat

63. Mississippi Hot Dog Steamboat

64. Jingle Bells

65. Dreidel Song

66. The Bears Went Over the Mountain

This note gets 3 counts.

©2015 C. Harvey Publications All Rights Reserved.

67. Scotland's Burning: A Round

68. Old MacDonald

Stay in third position while you pick first finger up.

Shift back on the D string.

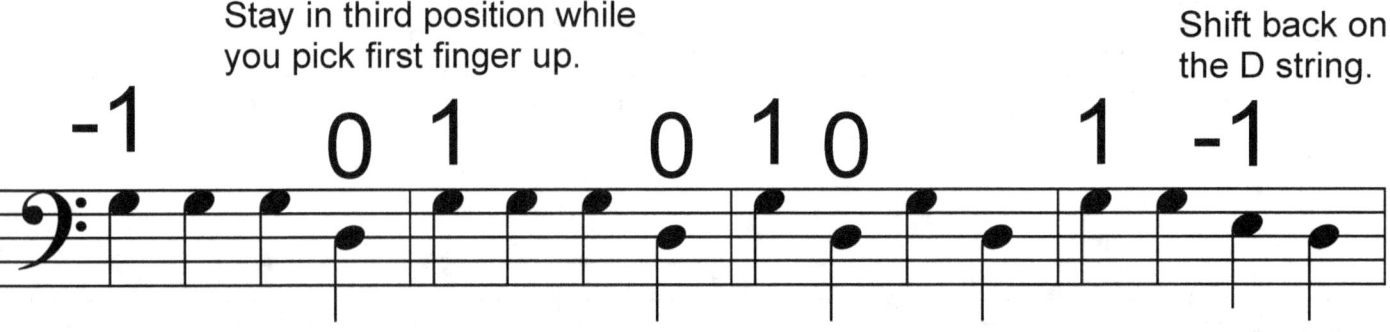

69. London Bridge

70. Cotton-Eyed Joe

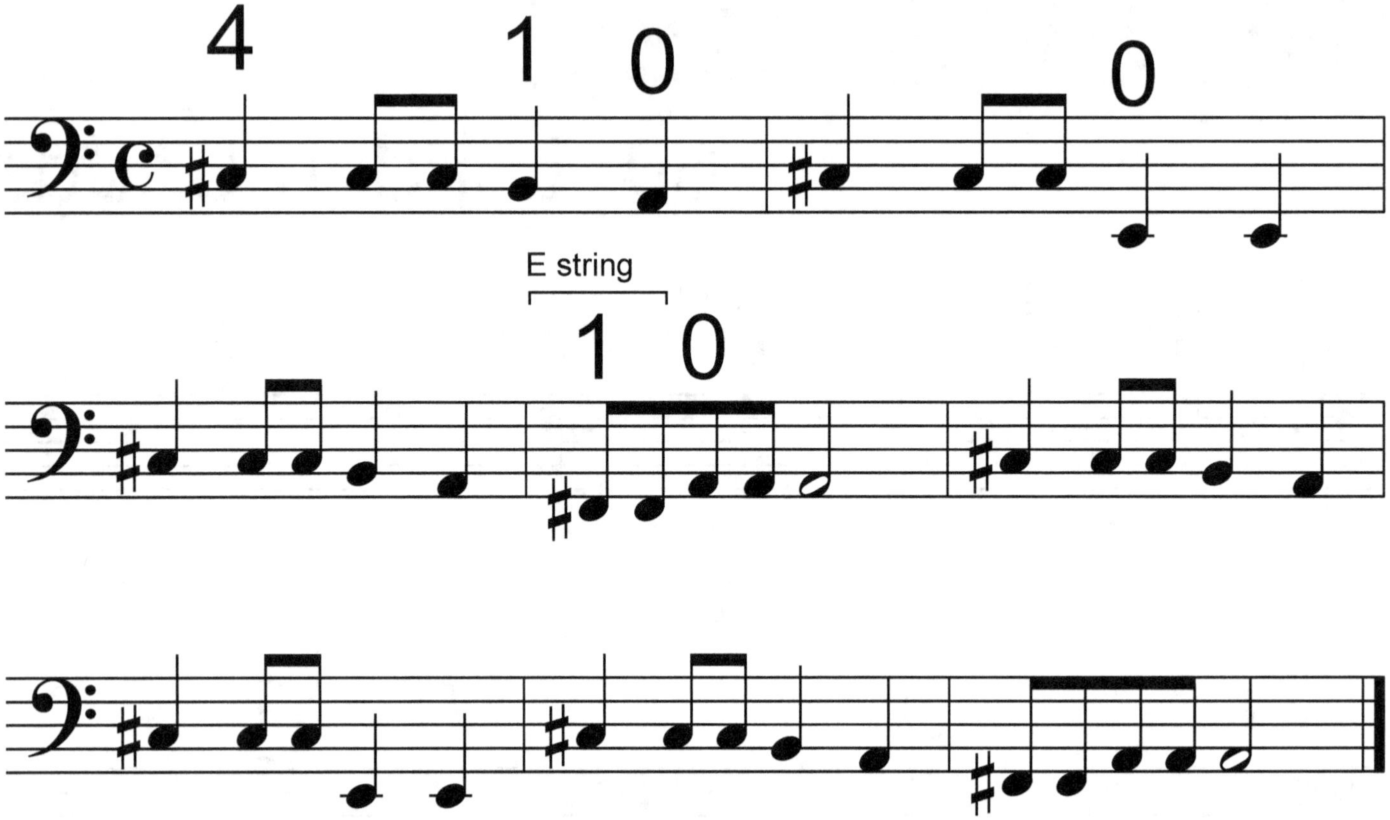

71. Mississippi Hot Dog Joe

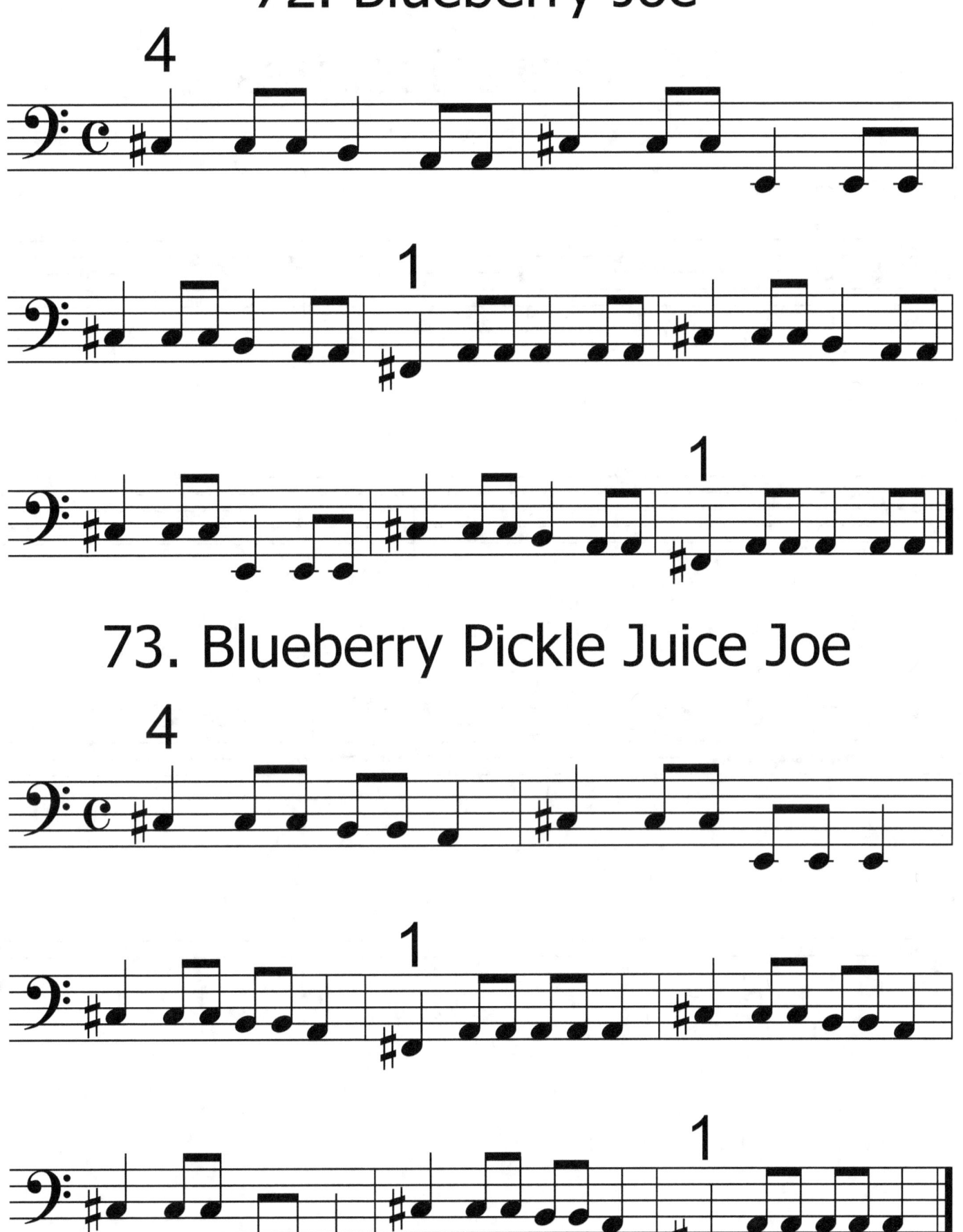

74. Frere Jacques

1.

2.
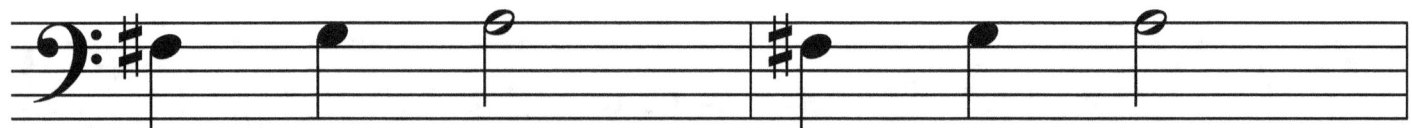

3.

4.

75. E and F♯ on the E string

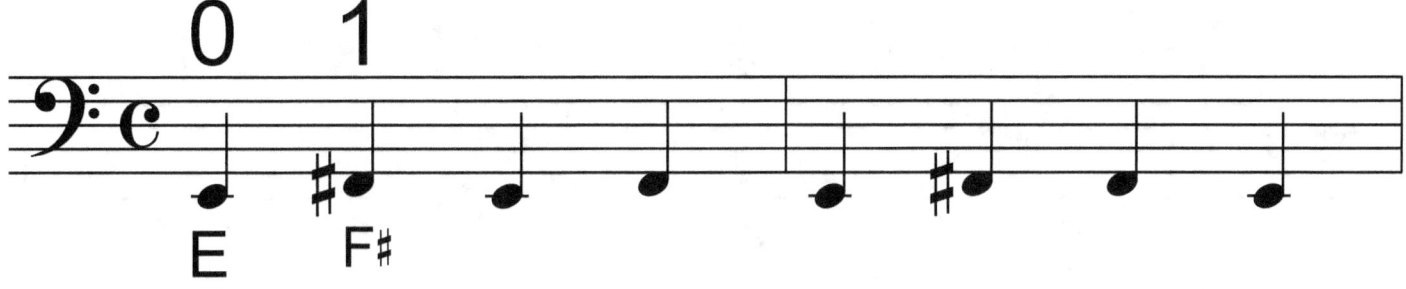

76. E, F♯, and G♯ on the E string

©2015 C. Harvey Publications All Rights Reserved.

77. E, F#, G#, and A on the E string

78. E, F#, G#, A, and B on the E string

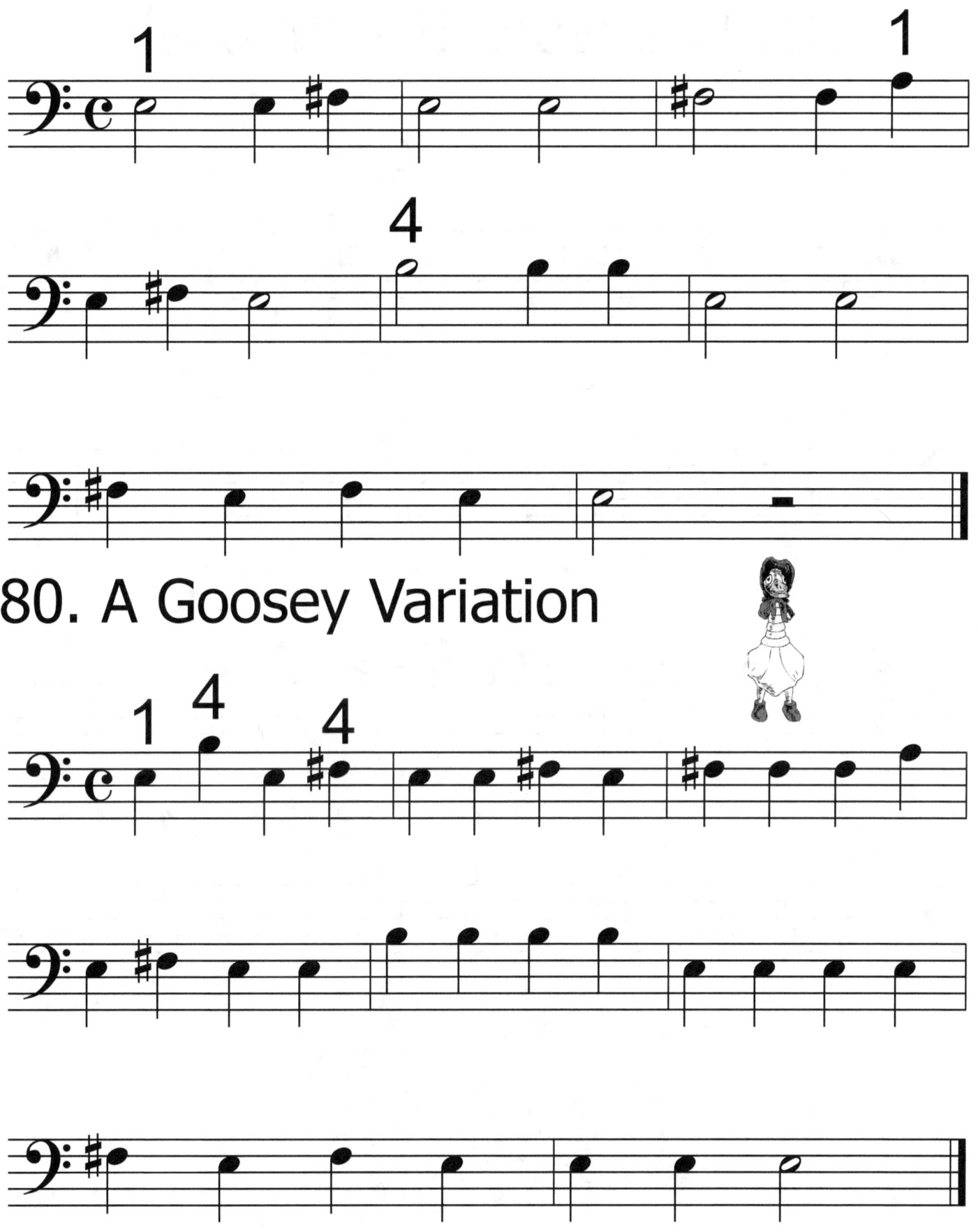

81. Pop Goes the Weasel

82. French Folk Song Harmony (to play with Violins)

83. French Folk Song Melody

84. An Anonymous Allegro

85. G and A on the G String

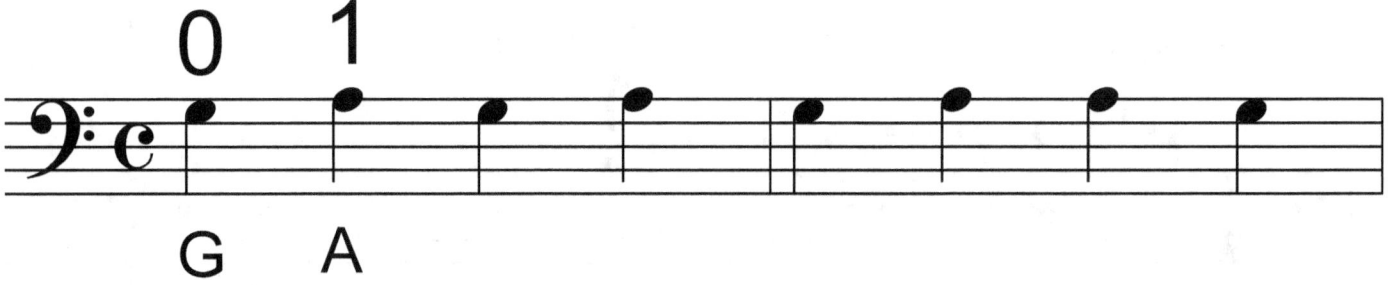

86. G, A, and B on the G String

Learning the Bass, Book One

87. G, A, B, and C on the G String

88. G, A, B, C, and D on the G String

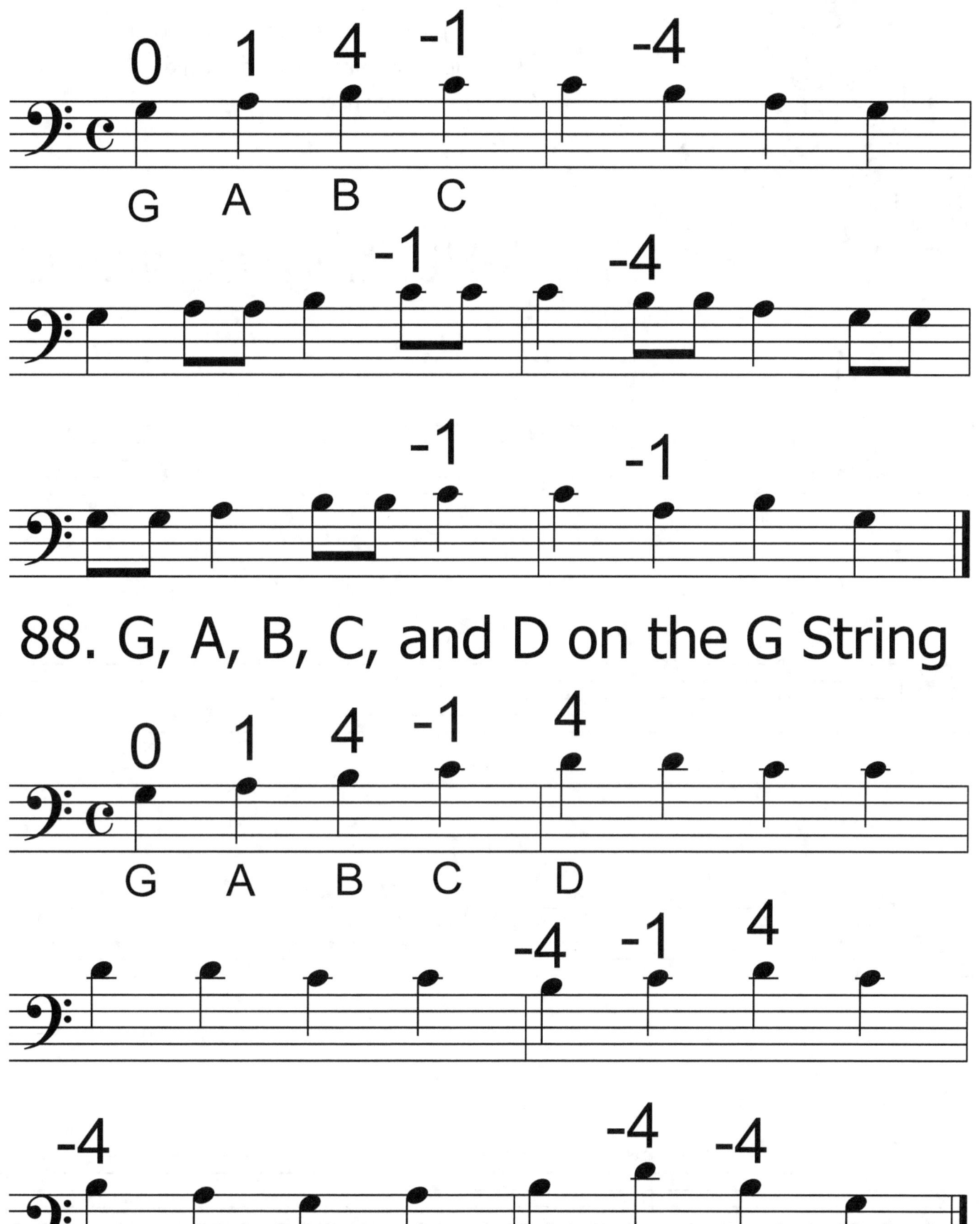

©2015 C. Harvey Publications All Rights Reserved.

A-hunting we will go, a-hunting we will go
We'll catch a pig and dance a little jig
And then we'll let him go!

89. A-Hunting We Will Go

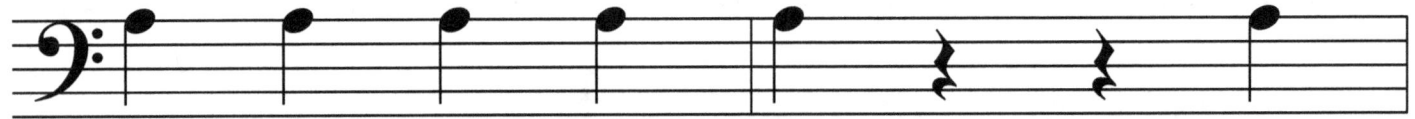

Learning the Bass, Book One

90. River Train

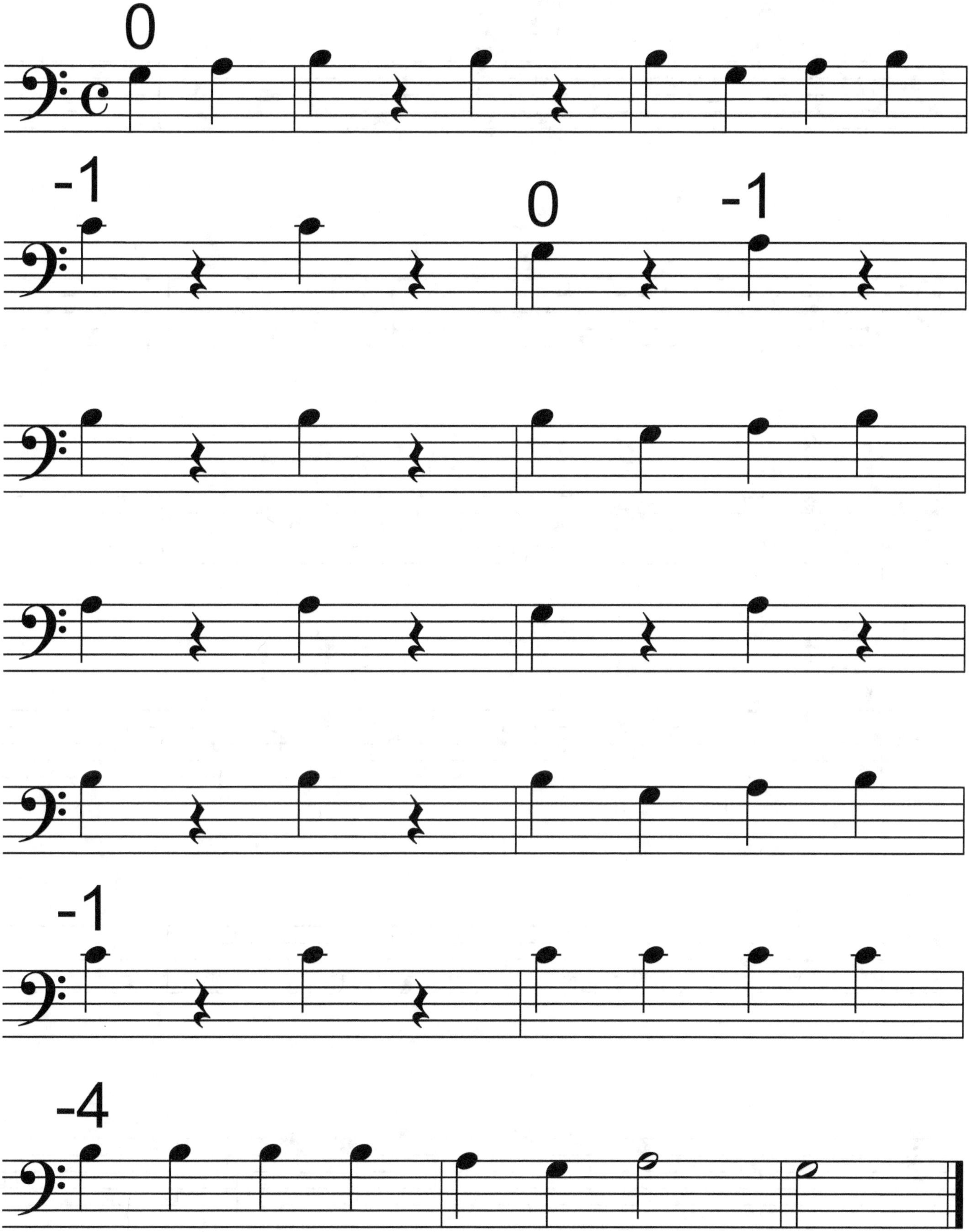

91. Dvorak's Largo

92. Violas and Cellos Learn C and D

93. Violas and Cellos Learn C, D, and E

94. 2nd Finger F Natural (♮)

95. F♮ and G

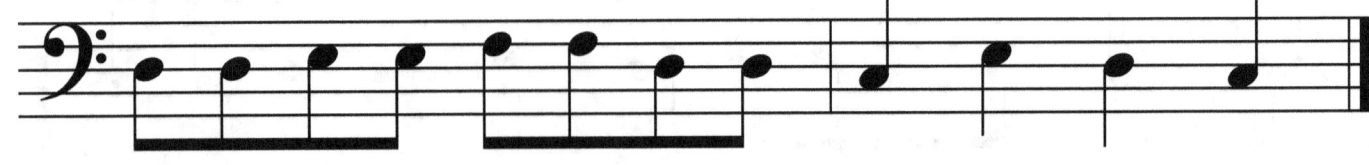

96. Hammer Ring

97. Won't You Ring, Old Hammer?

98. Yankee Doodle

99. The Spider Song

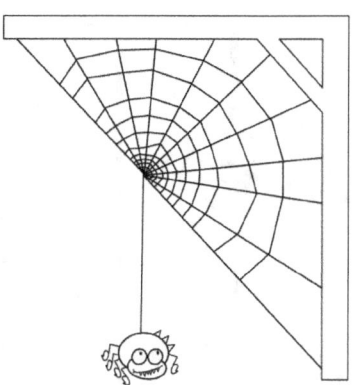

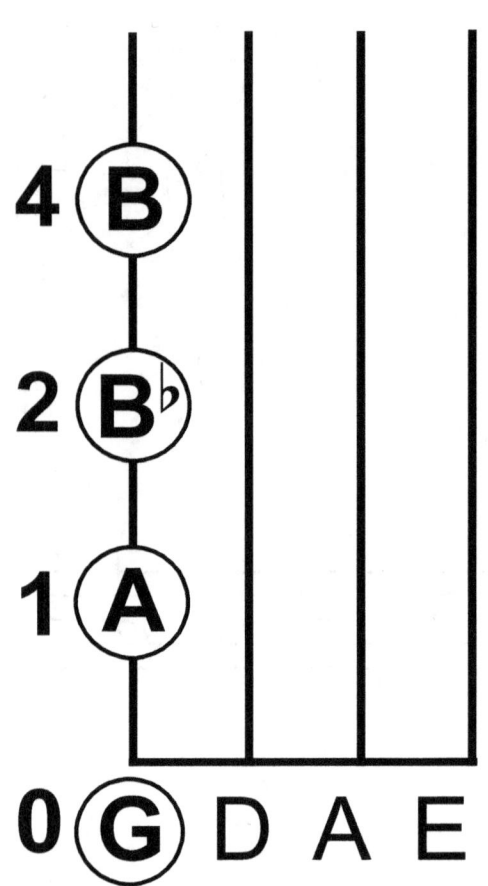
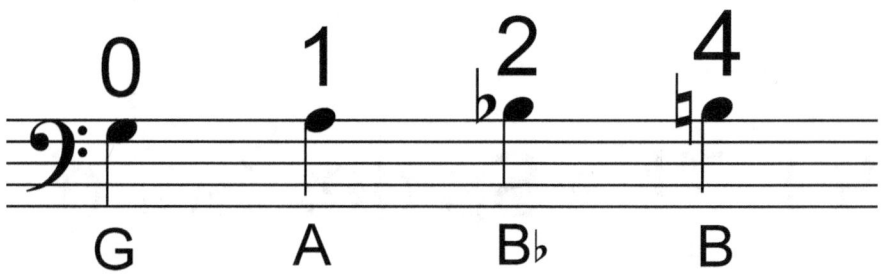

G string

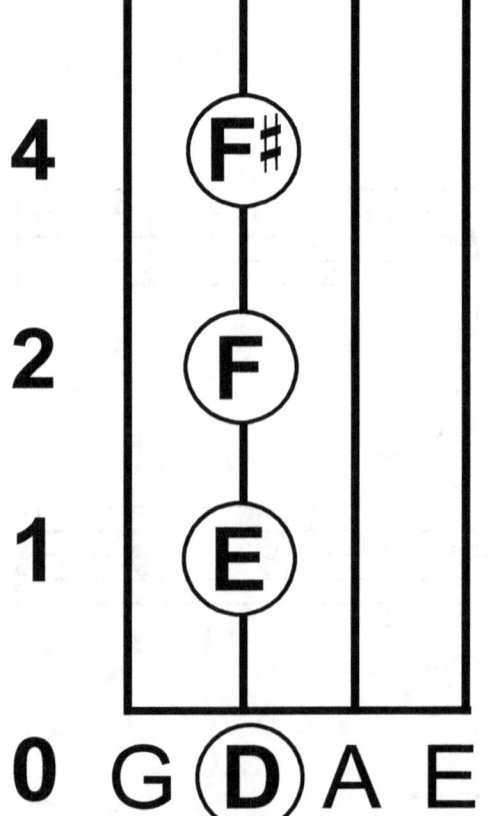
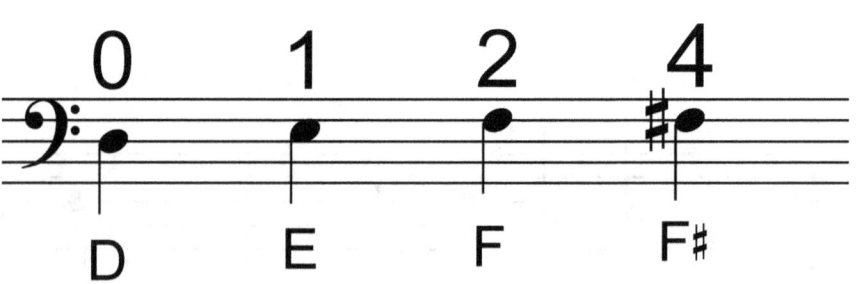

D string

Learning the Bass, Book One 77

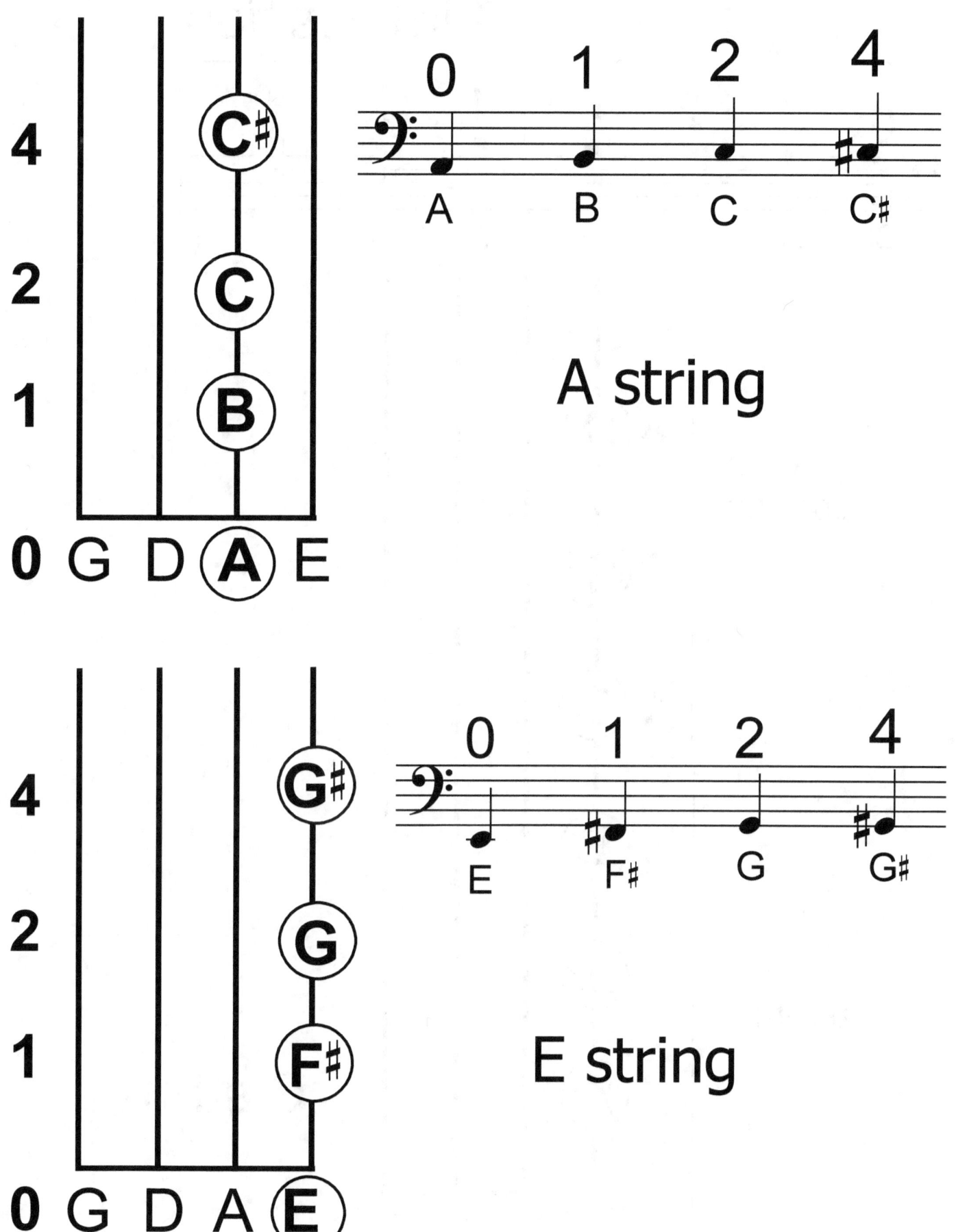

Third Position

G string

Learning the Bass, Book One

Third Position

D string

www.ingramcontent.com/pod-product-compliance
Lightning Source LLC
Chambersburg PA
CBHW051422070526
44584CB00023B/3534